Holly Celebrates Valentine's Day

Written by Kimberly Kendall-Drucker

Illustrated by Kiara Naybab

Copyright © 2022. Kimberly Kendall-Drucker

All rights reserved. No portion of this book may be reproduced in any form without expressed written permission from Just Write Publications except as permitted by U.S. copyright law.

No part of this publication may be reproduced, stored in a retrieval system, or transmitted in any form or by any means, electronic, mechanical, photocopying, recording, or otherwise, without written permission from the author. For information regarding permission, visit kimberlykendalldrucker.com.

ISBN: 978-0-578-35455-2 (hardback)
ISBN: 978-0-578-35456-9 (paperback)
Library of Congress Control Number: 2022900489

For My Valentine

Larry Drucker

For My Nieces and Nephews

Courtney, Kayla, Lauren, Jaylen, Angel, Roman, Sincere, Lennox, Banks, Miles, Marlie, Bella, and Warren

Holidays are special days
Spread all throughout the year.
And most of them are festive,
As they fill our hearts with cheer.

Some "Holly-Days" are SPRING-time days
Some WINTER, SUMMER, FALL,
And since my name is Holly
I just celebrate them all.

Juneteenth Picnic

FEBRUARY

S	M	T	W	T	F	S
		1	2	3	4	5
6	7	8	9	10	11	12
13	14	15	16	17	18	19
20	21	22	23	24	25	26
27	28					

Some Holly-Days are sacred,
And some Holly-Days are merry,
But the sweetest Holly-Day of all
Happens in **February**.

It is a day when we eat chocolates
From a box shaped like a **heart**,
Yet so many people wonder
When **Valentine's Day** got its start.

Long ago a man named
Served as emperor of the land,
And he made some laws and policies
The people could not stand.

He decreed to all his people
Soldiers' weddings were forbidden.
But the soldiers married anyway -
And they just kept it hidden.

A Priest whose name was **Valentine**
Helped soldiers and their wives.
He performed their secret weddings,
So they could start their married lives.

But when Emperor Claudius found out
What Valentine had done
He threw him deep into a dungeon
Where he could not see the sun.

But one day a kind and lovely girl
Brought him some bread and water
And just like that, Priest Valentine
Fell for his jailer's daughter!

He wrote her beautiful love letters
He asked her, "**Please be mine**."
And beneath his words of love and hope
Signed, *From your Valentine.*

One **February the 14th**
He sent her his last note,
And today we all still celebrate
The letters that priest wrote.

The priest became **Saint Valentine.**
And from that day 'til this
We send Valentines to our loved ones
And seal them with a kiss.

Valentine's Day is set aside for love
And flowers, hearts, and candy
A day we show those we are closest to
We think they are just dandy.

We do nice things for our parents
We give cards to our classmates
And someday when we are all grown up,
We'll **celebrate** on dates.

Some go to lavish restaurants
For a fancy bite to eat.
Some give their sweethearts chocolates
As an extra special treat.

Some people send red roses
Others send a teddy bear
And kids give school friends candy hearts
To let them know they care.

A perfect day to love your parents
A festive day to love your friends
If you need to say I'm sorry,
It's a day to make amends.

Oh! We love our friends and family
And while we surely hope they know it –
There's no better day than Valentine's
To tell them and to show it.

But if you're not sure how to show it
There's one sure thing that you could do
Just write a letter like Saint Valentine
And sign it, **I love you**.

The End

Next in the Series...

Holly Celebrates Earth Day
Holly Celebrates Juneteenth
Holly Celebrates Independence Day

About the Author

Kimberly Kendall-Drucker lives in Charlotte, North Carolina with her husband Larry and Persian Princess – her kitty, Zuzu. She loves reading, and her books are her friends. Her favorite childhood books are *A Wrinkle in Time, Are You There God? It's Me, Margaret, and Roll of Thunder Hear My Cry*. Kimberly reads a book a week – sometimes two. She is committed to increasing literacy instilling a love for reading in children - because *readers are leaders*.

Kimberly loves Uno, chocolate-peanut butter ice cream, and graphic tees. She is an incredibly competitive Scrabble player, and Jeopardy is her favorite TV show. While some people are outdoorsy, Kimberly is decidedly indoorsy - although few things please her more than a day at the beach. She often engages in marathon phone calls with her Best Girl and mother, Levones Chisholm and believes laugher is truly the best medicine. Last, but certainly not least, Kimberly's nieces and nephews are her pride and joy.

Holly Celebrates Valentine's Day is the second book in the *Holly Celebrates Series* and is Kimberly's third children's book.

To contact Kimberly or learn more about her, check out her website – kimberlykendalldrucker.com.

www.ingramcontent.com/pod-product-compliance
Lightning Source LLC
Chambersburg PA
CBHW061803290426

44109CB00030B/2925